CHILDREN'S
RIGHTS

Essential Issues

CHILDREN'S
RIGHTS

BY COURTNEY FARRELL

SAVE CHILDHOOD
SAVE CHILDRIGHTS

Content Consultant
Patrick Emerson
Associate Professor, Department of Economics
Oregon State University

ABDO
Publishing Company

CREDITS

Published by ABDO Publishing Company, 8000 West 78th Street,
Edina, Minnesota 55439. Copyright © 2010 by Abdo Consulting
Group, Inc. International copyrights reserved in all countries. No
part of this book may be reproduced in any form without written
permission from the publisher. The Essential Library™ is a
trademark and logo of ABDO Publishing Company.

Printed in the United States of America,
North Mankato, Minnesota
102009
012010

 PRINTED ON RECYCLED PAPER

Editor: Amy Van Zee
Copy Editor: Paula Lewis
Interior Design and Production: Nicole Brecke
Cover Design: Nicole Brecke

Library of Congress Cataloging-in-Publication Data
Farrell, Courtney.
  Children's rights / Courtney Farrell.
    p. cm. — (Essential issues)
  Includes bibliographical references.
  ISBN 978-1-60453-952-3
  1. Children's rights—Juvenile literature. 2. Child labor—Juvenile
literature. 3. Child slaves—Juvenile literature. 4. Child sexual
abuse—Juvenile literature. 5. Children—Legal status, laws, etc.—
Juvenile literature. I. Title.
  HQ789.F368 2010
  305.23086'942—dc22

                              2009029938

TABLE OF CONTENTS

*A child laborer turns bricks to be baked by the sun in Pakistan,
where millions of children are laborers.*

Ashiq's Story

Eleven-year-old Ashiq never played. He did not go to school, though he wanted to. He was five when he began working in a brick factory in Pakistan, sold into bonded labor to help pay off his family's debt. He received one day off per month. Every other day, he arrived at work in the dark at 2:00 a.m. He worked with his family and other bonded slaves—adults and children—until 8:00 a.m. Then they had a 30-minute break and returned to work until 6:00 p.m. Together, Ashiq and his family made the equivalent of $2.10 per day, but they were only paid if they could finish 1,000 bricks before quitting time.

Because there were no machines to help with the work, the bricks were all made by hand. Workers mixed the clay by adding water and stomping on it with their bare feet. They pressed the wet clay by hand into wooden molds. The hardest work came when the bricks dried. Even very small children carried stacks of bricks on their backs or balanced on top of their heads. The dry bricks shed a lot of irritating dust, which the children breathed in. The dust coated their faces and got in their eyes as they struggled barefoot across the rocky ground to the kiln where the bricks were fired. The kiln was fueled by

Bonded Labor Is Modern Slavery

In Asia, a poor family that needs a loan can sell themselves or their children into bonded labor, which is also called debt slavery. The practice is deceptive because a high-interest loan is given, but workers earn only pennies per day. They may never be able to pay off the loan. Sometimes entire families end up as debt slaves. If a parent who is a bonded laborer dies, his children inherit the debt. Because bonded workers are not allowed to quit their jobs, bonded labor is really a form of slavery.

Unaware Consumers

Consumers in the United States and other westernized countries may unwittingly contribute to the exploitation of children by purchasing products that were made using child labor. Inexpensive imported goods might be cheap for a reason; the workers who made them may not have been paid a fair wage. People want inexpensive goods, and workers in developing nations produce them. These workers are often desperate for jobs, so they and their children will accept low wages and poor working conditions just to survive.

wood, if wood could be found, but often it burned old tires or plastic trash. Toxic smoke billowed across the brickyard.

Rarely, a child would attempt to escape, but he would not get far. The perimeter of the brickyard was guarded, and malnutrition made the child weak. He would be quickly caught, beaten, and returned to work. Children in the brickyard did not live very long.

This is a true story, and the events described occurred in the recent past. Today, children all over the world work. Some work such long hours that they cannot attend school. In some of the worst examples of child labor, they work under wretched conditions, in extreme cold or heat, and without enough food or water. Some work in brickyards, toil underground in mines, or are chained to looms in rug factories. Some children are even forced into prostitution or used as soldiers in armed combat. But in other places, children work on farms or as household servants.

Children Have Rights

All children, no matter where they live, have basic human rights. They share the right to safety, the love of their families, adequate food and rest, and an education. They share the right to real childhoods, without being forced to marry or have sex before they are ready.

However, the way people view children's rights is dependent on their culture. For example, people in Western countries are likely to oppose child labor, arranged marriages of children, and the use of children as soldiers. But these practices are not always considered wrong in some other countries. So which rights should all children have regardless of the culture they live in? Nations are working together to answer this question and to establish laws that defend those rights.

UN Convention on the Rights of the Child

The United Nations Convention on the Rights of the Child (UNCRC) is an international treaty about the treatment of children. Countries that sign it agree to abide by its rules. The convention declares that children are individuals, not chattel.

Children gathered at the United Nations in Geneva, Switzerland, on June 12, 2008, to support World Day against Child Labor.

This means they are not property, even of their parents. They have the right to live with their parents and communities and to visit both parents if their parents are divorced. They have the right not to be exploited and to have their opinions taken into consideration. The convention also forbids capital punishment—the death penalty—for convicted criminals under the age of 18.

The UN has also created several related documents called optional protocols, which contain additional rules. Countries may choose to sign the main convention, but not the optional protocols. One optional protocol bans the use of children as soldiers, and another makes it illegal to sell children, force them into prostitution, or use their pictures in child pornography. The only member countries of the UN that have not signed the treaty are Somalia and the United States. Some say the United States has not done so because it fears that international law would overshadow U.S. state and federal laws.

Limited Rights Protect Children

Children do not have the same rights as adults. Many countries have commonsense limitations on the rights of children. Laws prevent them from risky behaviors such as driving cars, drinking alcohol, and fighting in wars.

Such laws ensure that children are educated and cared for. For example, in the United States, there is a legal limit on the number of hours a child can work. This limit applies to any type of work, whether the child is an actor or a dishwasher in a restaurant. The law was passed because people recognized the damage that long hours of work can do to young bodies and minds. The repetitive motions used in factory work or farmwork can leave kids with arthritis and tendonitis, painful disorders usually seen only in older people. Free time is also essential for a child's normal emotional and mental development. Unfortunately, laws written to protect children are difficult to enforce. Child workers are often hidden away in houses or behind locked doors in sweatshop factories.

Kathie Lee Gifford's Child Labor Scandal

When U.S. talk show host Kathie Lee Gifford lent her name to a line of low-cost women's clothing, she did not investigate the factories that made the clothes. In one Honduran factory, girls as young as 12 years old worked for 31 cents an hour. According to 15-year-old seamstress Wendy Diaz, workdays ranged between 13 and 22.5 hours long, and children worked seven days a week. Armed guards and barbed wire surrounded the factory, so bosses decided when workers could leave.

Gifford received a massive wave of negative publicity in 1996 for paying workers so little while netting more than $5 million herself. In her defense, she stated, "My first endorsement was for Kraft when I was 17, and I didn't think I had to go check out the cows."[1] New York labor activists staged street protests against her.

Finally, Gifford visited the factories. Gifford took measures to improve the working conditions there. She even became an activist against child labor herself, speaking before Congress and meeting with President Bill Clinton. As a result of the publicity, a White House task force signed an agreement with apparel manufacturers in the United States to improve working conditions in factories overseas. The agreement called for improvements, but it still allows workers as young as 14 to work 60-hour weeks for approximately a dollar a day.

Most people agree that daily household chores done before or after school are not damaging to children. In fact, the chores likely have a positive influence by teaching responsibility. Activists who work to end child labor are not opposed to children working at home on tasks such as cleaning their rooms, washing dishes, or doing chores on a family farm.

For example, on U.S. farms, children usually do chores such as feeding chickens or cleaning stalls, but they still go to school. This is not considered child labor. However, these children have very different lives from the children of some migrant farmworkers in the United States. Migrant farmworkers are poor laborers who travel year-round to find work on farms. These children often work long shifts on commercial farms and do not attend school. Many people consider this to be an unacceptable form of child labor.

What Are Sweatshops?

Sweatshops are factories where the working conditions are terrible and the pay is low. The name originally described dress-making shops in high-rise tenements where the rooms were sweltering. The term has widened to include factories where workers are exploited. Sweatshop owners and managers have been accused of refusing to pay wages, sexually harassing female workers, verbally and physically abusing workers, and using child labor.

WHY CHILDREN'S RIGHTS ARE VIOLATED

Money is one of the root causes of the violation of children's rights. Poverty makes families desperate. With no other options, hopeless parents may arrange marriages for young daughters or even sell children into bonded labor. Hu Xingdau, an economics professor at the Beijing Institute of Technology, wrote about child labor in China. He stated,

> *Most of the [child] work force comes from underdeveloped or poverty-stricken areas. Some children are even sold by their parents, who often don't have any idea of the [terrible] working conditions.* [2]

But not all adults who violate children's rights are poor. Some—such as sweatshop factory owners—are merely unscrupulous people who take advantage of vulnerable children in order to make a profit.

Another root cause for the violation of children's rights is a lack of education. Some say parents with low levels of education are likely to have large numbers of children, creating financial strain. Their children often leave school early to work at low-paying jobs that require little training and do not teach a trade. This creates a cycle in which poverty continues throughout generations.

In developed countries, children who work instead of attending school are often disadvantaged for their entire lives. These children may not be able to read well or at all. Because literacy is one of the basic skills required for any good job, working children who are not educated will have limited career choices when they reach adulthood.

THE HEART OF THE ISSUE

The situation is complicated by different cultural norms. For example, in remote areas of developing countries where indigenous communities survive by hunting, fishing, and gardening, children are often needed to perform labor. In such places, village children work alongside their parents while learning traditional skills. These children are expected to contribute and would likely be considered lazy if they did not work. Unless the

Birth Control

Birth control prevents pregnancy, so it allows women to choose whether they will have children. In the United States, birth control can be obtained from doctors or clinics, but it may not be available to women in developing countries. Without birth control, a woman could have more children than she can support and she and her children could end up in poverty. This, in turn, puts her children at risk for being victims of child labor.

village became rapidly developed, a lack of schooling would not be a crippling disadvantage in such cultures because the children would have spent their childhoods learning the skills to survive as an adult.

The world contains many cultures, and with each culture comes a different belief system about the role of children. In regard to children's rights, there are many questions. How does one define the rights of children? Who has the right to define children's rights? Are there different expectations of children in different cultures? Are there universal rights that all humans are given no matter their age? International aid organizations are uniting in an attempt to resolve these very issues. But when it comes to children's rights, there may be more questions than answers. ⌐

Former child laborers demonstrated against child labor in New Delhi, India, on November 8, 1996.

Laborers work in a bakery in ancient Rome.

HISTORY OF
CHILD LABOR

*I*n the distant past, children were considered chattel of their fathers. During the Roman Empire (27 BCE–476 CE), extended families lived together under the authority of the father or the grandfather. Although abuse was rare, any member of the family could be beaten, sold into slavery, or even legally killed by the family authority. Any money earned by the sons, even once they reached adulthood, belonged to their father. Girls and women worked at home, but they were rarely paid.

By the Middle Ages (400–1400), children had gained a few more rights. Fathers could no longer legally have their sons or daughters executed, but they still ruled over their lives. On medieval farms, children were expected to help as soon as they were able, but they had some free time to play with friends and participate in seasonal celebrations. Most families lived in villages where everyone knew their neighbors. Older children were often apprenticed to local craftsmen to learn a trade. This close-knit society provided a measure of protection for working children. They were

Social Classes

In the Middle Ages, people were divided into classes: peasants, clergy, and lords. Children belonged to whatever class their parents were in. A child of a peasant could never hope to become a lord, although he might learn a trade and make a fair living. That is one of the main differences between medieval society and modern society. Today, people are not bound to remain in the class into which they were born. Those who work hard and earn good grades in school can win a scholarship to a college, earn a degree, or become wealthy, no matter what their social class may have been at birth. Some people may even become successful without an advanced education.

supervised by parents or neighbors, who usually had their best interests at heart. The Industrial Revolution would change all that.

The Industrial Revolution

The Industrial Revolution was a period of technological advancement and large-scale industrialization. In Europe and the United States, it occurred approximately between 1760 and 1850, but in many developing countries it is still in progress. In such places, much work is not yet mechanized, and heavy labor is often performed by people or draft animals.

In order for any society to develop technology, its farmers must be able to feed themselves and have enough food left over for nonfarming families to purchase. The food surplus that Europe experienced near the beginning of the Industrial Revolution allowed people to spend their time on pursuits other than farming. Some became merchants, while others invented machines and built factories.

More food also meant the human population could grow, and it did. The surplus population poured into cities to look for jobs. The poor crowded into small apartments without indoor plumbing or running water. On farms, large families were an advantage, because many people were needed to work the land. But in cities, food had to be bought to feed each person, so numerous offspring became a burden. Children had to find full-time jobs to help their families survive.

CHILDREN SUFFERED IN FACTORIES

During the Industrial Revolution, trades such as spinning and weaving became mechanized and were transferred to factories. Previously, weaving had been done mostly by women and children who worked part-time in their homes. Later, children took jobs making cloth in textile mills. They tended large, clattering machines for 12 to 18 hours at a time. Factory owners preferred to hire children rather than adult men because the children were easier to control. They did not complain as

Workhouses

In 1576, an act of the British parliament initiated poorhouses to aid the needy. The act required jobless people to be provided with work by their communities and given raw materials to work with, such as wool. By 1834, the poor had greatly increased in number, and taxpayers thought that payments of money and goods encouraged laziness. Workhouses were designed as a solution. Workhouses were large, bleak factory buildings where the poor could go to live if they had no other option. There, everyone had to work, even young children. Families were split up, as men, women, and children were housed in separate wings. Working conditions were intentionally terrible as an incentive for the poor to support themselves.

much about poor working conditions and did not demand high wages.

Job site safety was not a priority, and some of the machines were designed with exposed gears that could crush a hand or a foot. The worst abuses occurred when working children were separated from their families. They were handed over to factory owners, who fed them poorly and worked them for long hours.

Reform Begins in Britain

In 1802, and again in 1819, the British parliament passed acts limiting the workday of children to no more than 12 hours per day. These laws were not well enforced, however, and many young children still worked 16 to 18 hours a day. At that time, it was not unusual to see children as young as three in the workforce.

Among the British public, sentiment against child labor gradually increased. A group of Evangelical Christians formed Short-Time Committees that worked to change the law. Short-Time Committees wanted children under the age of nine to be banned from working at all. They pushed for a ten-hour day to be enforced for older children.

*During the Industrial Revolution, factories became mechanized.
Many workers were needed to run the machines.*

Around 1840, these people found a powerful ally
in their fellow Evangelical, Lord Ashley, Earl of
Shaftesbury.

When Lord Ashley learned about the abuse
of child workers, he said he was "astonished and
disgusted" and became a passionate reformer.[1] Lord
Ashley and his supporters began the Children's
Employment Commission in 1840. The commission
interviewed many children about their working

conditions in mines, textile mills, and as apprentices. Lord Ashley hoped to use the reports to sway public opinion against child labor. In 1842, the Children's Employment Commission sent R. H. Franks to investigate the working conditions of children employed in collieries, or coal mines, in Scotland.

THE COAL MINES ACT OF 1842

In the nineteenth century, all mines were dug by hand, so passages were cramped and narrow. Mines were often flooded, and workers had to wade through dirty water. Each man was paid by the amount of coal he collected per day, but he had to pay the colliers—people who hauled coal to the surface—out of his own wages.

Men brought their wives and children into the mines as colliers to save money. Though children could more easily navigate the tunnels

---

The Life of a Collier

In one portion of Franks's report, he cited interviews with child workers, including Janet Cumming, who worked as a collier. In 1842, the girl described her job. About herself, she stated, "Works with father; has done so two years. . . . The roof is very low; I have to bend my back and legs, and the water comes frequently up to the calves of my legs; has no likening for the work; father makes me like it . . . often obliged to scramble out when bad air was in the pit. Father lately got crushed by a big coal falling."[2]

than adults, the passages were still not large enough for even a child to stand up in. Colliers had to crawl, pulling their carts by harnesses tied around their hips. Sometimes several children drew a single cart, with some pushing and the others pulling. By the end of a shift in the mines, children were coated with toxic black coal dust. Mine workers often died young from a combination of overwork, malnutrition, and black lung disease.

When the reports of Franks were released, the British public was shocked. Lord Ashley successfully gained support for his 1842 Coal Mines Act. Women and children were banned from working in mines.

Lord Ashley became the Seventh Earl of Shaftesbury in 1851. Although he created many "ragged schools" that taught poor children for free, he could not completely eliminate child labor.[3]

Black Lung Disease

Black lung disease is caused by inhaling coal dust, which turns the inside of a miner's lungs black instead of the normal pink color. The disease can cause difficulty breathing. It usually affects miners over the age of 50—young people who are affected usually do not live long.

A Lewis Hine photograph shows two boys working at a glass factory in Indiana in 1908.

CHILD LABOR IN THE UNITED STATES

In 1900, some U.S. children were in school, but many others worked long hours. According to the 1900 census, approximately 2 million children were subjected to difficult labor. In rural areas, children picked cotton, mined, and farmed. In cities, they worked in mills and on the streets selling newspapers or shining shoes. The high humidity inside mill factories was particularly damaging to the health of children. Respiratory problems such as tuberculosis were rampant. Because children were paid lower wages than adults, factories often hired children, though the streets were full of unemployed men.

U.S. CHILD LABOR REFORMER

Lewis Hine was born in Wisconsin in 1874. He grew up to be a small, shy man who worked as a teacher in New York City. Around 1904, the National Child Labor Committee (NCLC) was mobilizing the movement against child labor in the United States. Hine became an investigative photographer for the NCLC and

Tuberculosis in Mill Children

Tuberculosis (TB) is a disease that spreads when infected people cough bacteria into the air. TB mainly affects the lungs, but it can also spread to other organs and cause serious harm. In mills, windows were kept closed because high humidity was needed to keep machine parts from breaking. The workers kept breathing the same muggy air. Exhaustion and poor nutrition made their bodies' resistance to the disease low, and TB spread quickly. The survival rate of mill children was only half that of schoolchildren.

TB thrives under conditions of poverty and urbanization, mainly because of crowding. Although TB declined with better living conditions in the last 50 years, it is now on the rise again. HIV-infected people are likely to contract and spread TB. Many strains of TB can be cured with antibiotics, but antibiotic-resistant strains have arisen. Worldwide, up to half the population is infected, but immune systems of otherwise healthy people can suppress the infection. A vaccine is available for children in areas where infection rates are high.

documented the conditions of child workers.

Investigation of child labor was a dangerous job. Factory owners were aware of the growing feelings against child labor, and they did not want any publicity. These owners were usually wealthy and influential men, and some of them arranged for investigators to be harassed or jailed.

To gain entrance into the factories, Lewis Hine often pretended to be a fire inspector, an industrial photographer, or an insurance salesman. He said he was interested in the equipment but instead focused his camera on the child workers. Hine asked questions about accidents and noted unsafe situations such as small children leaning over the exposed gears of moving machinery.

Hine's photographs helped publicize the poor working conditions in the factories. Pictures

Avondale Mine Disaster

On September 6, 1869, a fire at the Avondale Colliery in Pennsylvania trapped the miners and used up all of the oxygen in the tunnels. Five boys between the ages of 12 and 17 were suffocated, as were 105 men. The body of one father was found with his arm still around his son's.

Mining accidents such as these occurred as a result of explosions, cave-ins, falling coal from walls, and smothering from falling into the coal chute. Today, mining is safer than it was, but miners are still at risk for accidents.

showed how small the children in the mills were compared to the large, dangerous machines. Hine captured the grime and exhaustion on the faces of young miners. Almost all of them were underweight, with dark circles under their eyes. Many looked worried and sad. People who had imagined child laborers working happily alongside their parents on idyllic farms saw the reality of the situation, and they did not approve.

Child labor laws were passed in 1916 and 1918. But both times, the Supreme Court declared them unconstitutional. In 1924, Congress passed a constitutional amendment banning child labor, but the bill was never ratified by state lawmakers. The labor of children was profitable to many powerful people, and they would not give up their inexpensive workforce without a fight.

Roosevelt Bans Child Labor

In 1938, U.S. President Franklin Delano Roosevelt signed the Fair Labor Standards Act. The act set minimum wages and limited the number of hours on a work shift. But most importantly, it prohibited children under the age of 16 from working in mines and factories. The U.S. secretary of labor could also deem certain jobs hazardous. These jobs were then off-limits to children under 18. The law still allowed children to work in agricultural jobs, but in 1946, this loophole was closed and U.S. children were sent to school.

This 1908 photograph shows two young boys working
as drivers in a West Virginia coal mine.

Young people in the United States have more rights and privileges than their peers in many countries.

RIGHTS OF U.S. TEENS

ost young people in the United States only become concerned about their legal rights at home if there is a problem. For example, during family conflicts, angry parents have attempted to charge their teens rent or kick them out of the house entirely. Depending on the child's age, this is not always legal. Parents have a responsibility to support their children until they turn 18. If the parents do not, they can be charged with neglect and even go to jail. This means parents must pay for basic food, shelter, and clothing, and they cannot ask to be reimbursed later.

In return, young people have certain responsibilities. One is to obey their parents, as long as the parents do not ask them to do anything illegal or immoral.

Children and teens must also comply with curfew and be home by the appointed hour. Curfews are usually written into law by each town or city. Teens out past curfew may be charged fines or get in trouble with the police. Also, parents may insist on a curfew that is earlier than the legal one.

Abuse and Neglect

Young people who are the victims of abuse or neglect can contact the police for help by dialing 911. Most likely, police will enlist the aid of social workers to investigate the charges. This does not always mean that the child will be removed from the home, especially if he or she does not want to be. If abuse or neglect is severe, a foster home can be provided until experts determine that the family is ready to be reunited. In the worst cases, abusive parents will be prosecuted and may go to jail. If the non-abusive parent is unable or not willing to protect the child, the child is placed in foster care, with adoptive families, or with relatives.

SCHOOL IS NOT OPTIONAL

Children in the United States are required to attend school through eighth grade. Parents who do not enroll their children in school or cannot prove that they are homeschooling their children adequately can face charges of neglect. In school, students are expected to respect teachers and school property. In many districts, parents of minors who damage school property have to pay for the damage.

Realistically, any adolescent who quits school after eighth grade does not have a bright future. As the world's population increases, competition for good jobs becomes more fierce. A high school diploma is a minimum requirement for most entry-level jobs. People without diplomas are relegated to low-paying jobs in labor or service industries. For a comfortable lifestyle with a little extra money for travel, hobbies, or other recreation, a college degree is now becoming essential. Students who dream of large homes and luxury cars should plan on staying in school even longer. It takes postgraduate work to prepare for a professional career with a large income, such as in medicine or the law. Fortunately, scholarships and financial aid are available to help students pay college tuition.

No Freedom of Religion for Minors

In the United States, minors have no freedom of religion. This may seem unfair to young people who are familiar with the constitutional right to freedom of religion. However, this right applies only to adults. Parents have the right to insist that their child be raised in their own religion, even if the child does not agree. Once minors turn 18, their parents can no longer force them to attend religious services.

Schools have no right to limit students' religious expression as long as that expression stays within the school dress code. For example, students may wear crosses, Stars of

Protection of Minority Religions

In 2002, Rebecca Moreno was suspended from Waxahachie High School in Texas for wearing a pentagram. A pentagram, which is a five-pointed star, is the symbol of her Wiccan religion. Wicca is a neo-pagan religion. It is based on respecting nature and views humans, animals, and Earth as sacred. Wicca acknowledges both male and female aspects of divinity.

Moreno argued that her right to wear the pentagram was protected under the First Amendment. High school officials disagreed. They believed the pentagram was a symbol of devil worship, as one of the Wiccan gods is horned and is often mistaken for the devil. The Moreno family hired an attorney, but the school district superintendent resolved the issue by deciding that even minority religions are protected by school board policy. Rebecca was then allowed to openly wear her pentagram. In other states, including Michigan and Indiana, judges have upheld the right of Wiccan students to wear pentagrams.

Sometimes schools enforce dress codes to help maintain order. The dress code can go so far as to require a school uniform.

David, head scarves, or pentacles as expressions of their faiths. This is considered part of their First Amendment rights, which guarantee the right to practice one's own religion and speak freely.

Schools Can Enforce Dress Codes

Gang members often identify themselves by wearing symbols on their clothes. Because gang activity is violent and disruptive, some schools have banned certain insignia on clothing, including some sports team logos. Because these messages are not religious, they can be legally banned by school authorities. Some schools have gone so far as to ban all hats or all clothing in colors associated with gangs.

Students often disagree with these policies, believing they go too far. The best way for students who oppose school policy to make a change is by working respectfully with administrators.

Is Spanking Legal?

Corporal punishment is the infliction of pain as a form of discipline. It may take the form of spanking, but it also includes more severe punishments. In the United States, laws about the legality of spanking vary. In most places, parents may spank their own children as long as they do not leave any visible marks such as bruises or cuts.

Corporal punishment was historically used in Europe, especially in English boarding schools. Now the practice is illegal in most European nations. It is also illegal in many African countries. Restricted corporal punishment is legal not only in the United States but also in Canada and some Asian countries.

In some U.S. schools, especially in the South, it is still legal to discipline children by paddling, or striking them with a stick or a whip. However, paddling in schools has been banned in 29 states.

The practice is rare for another reason, too. Adults who administer corporal punishment place themselves at risk of legal consequences, especially if the child is not their own. If a disagreement went to court, a judge would enlist the help of doctors and child development experts to determine if child abuse had occurred. Teachers do not want to put themselves at risk of being found guilty of a crime. Because of this, most schools in states where paddling is legal use it sparingly or not at all.

Students' Rights in School

In order for police to search a person, a home, or a vehicle, they

Some schools allow corporal punishment. This teacher's desk
includes a paddle and a switch for disciplining students.

need either a warrant or "probable cause"—a sign
of illegal activity. For example, a small amount of
marijuana visible in the ashtray of a car counts as
probable cause to search the entire car.

Schools have much more leeway to legally
search students for drugs, weapons, or other
contraband than police on the street. Students can
have no expectation of privacy in school lockers.
Administrators can legally bring in drug-sniffing
dogs and search every locker.

Students also have fewer rights of free speech
in their schools than they do on the street. Schools

do have the right to limit discussion of sex, drugs, or violence, and this includes writing in school newspapers or on hallway posters.

Relationships Can Be Legislated

To protect young people from sexual exploitation by adults, state laws set a minimum age of consent. This is the age at which a person can legally agree to have sex. Sex with a person younger than that age is always a crime, even if the younger person consents. The age of consent is either 16 or 18, depending on the state.

This law could affect teens even if they are dating someone in their own high school. For example, a freshman girl of 15 dating a senior boy of 18 would be in violation of the law if the relationship became sexual. Legal problems would only be likely if the girl or her parents initiated a lawsuit. In that case, they would have to prove the couple had sex, which might not be easy. The parents also might initiate a lawsuit if their daughter became pregnant.

Some judges may treat underage girls as victims, even if they consent to have sex with a boy of their own age. In these cases, only the boy may end up in trouble with the law.

GLBT Teens Have Equal Rights

Gay, lesbian, bisexual, and transgender (GLBT) teens have the same rights and protections under the law as any other teenagers. They have the right to be free from discrimination both at home and at school. GLBT teens also have the right to date anyone they wish, as long as that person is not an adult. Laws about age of consent still apply to same-sex couples.

Contraception for Underage Girls

Whether teenage girls should have the right to freely acquire contraception, or birth control, is a matter of dispute. Some health clinics will provide birth control for underage girls. The services are provided on a sliding scale, so teens without much money will pay a very low fee. Such clinics also provide

Teen Suicide

Suicide is the third-leading cause of death for those between the ages of 15 and 24. Factors that contribute to a young person's risk of suicide include substance abuse, depression, family instability, and trouble coming to terms with sexual orientation. Up to 30 percent of all teen suicides are by gay teens. Adults may try to help suicidal teens by giving them lectures on the reasons they have to live, but this approach generally does not work. An understanding person who listens can be of assistance. Professional treatment is also helpful and may include therapy and medication.

counseling and information on preventing pregnancy and sexually transmitted diseases. Their services are confidential, meaning they will not release information to anyone, including parents.

Some conservative organizations oppose this practice, believing that parents should always be informed if a teen is having sex. And some doctors have pledged not to provide contraceptives to unmarried teenagers at all.

Abortions for Teens

Controversy surrounds the question of abortion rights for teens. People disagree as to whether abortions should be allowed and whether parents need to be informed. U.S. law states that the female, no matter what her age, can decide if she wants to have an abortion or continue the pregnancy. No one is allowed to decide for her,

Protecting Vulnerable Citizens

The legal right to an abortion is a complicated and much-debated issue around the world. In terms of children's rights, when a teen girl considers an abortion the rights of two children are at stake—the mother and the baby. Those who believe that a woman's right to choose is of high value argue that abortion should be legal. Those who believe that society must protect the rights of its most vulnerable citizens, such as the unborn, say that abortion should be illegal.

not even her parents or the baby's father, though they might pressure her.

If a pregnant girl wants an abortion without informing her parents, she can apply for a judicial bypass. This is an order from a judge that declares the girl is able to have an abortion without her parents' consent. Sometimes girls fear violence if they tell their parents they are pregnant, so they may choose to keep the matter private. On the other hand, abortions can lead to medical problems such as infection or bleeding, so it may be risky for a girl to have an abortion without the knowledge of at least one of her parents.

If a girl has a baby, she cannot be forced to give it up for adoption, no matter her age. If a girl insists on keeping her baby, either her parents or state social workers help her raise the child. Some schools encourage

Sex Education

The topic of sex education is a hotly debated issue. Many schools choose to include sex education as part of their health and wellness courses. Teachers may instruct students about sexually transmitted diseases, contraception, and pregnancy. But some parents do not want their children to learn about these topics in school. They would rather teach their children these things themselves. In such cases, some schools offer opt-out policies that allow parents to choose to remove their child from the class.

young mothers to stay in school by allowing them to bring their babies to class. Authorities fear that a lack of an education could negatively affect the girl's future.

Many U.S. teens struggle with trying to find their own identity while living under the authority of one or more parents. On one hand, they may feel independent. On the other, U.S. law places them under the care of their parents or guardians until they reach the age of 18. Issues such as abortion, sexuality, dating, and curfews can be sources of contention for teens and their parents. But overall, U.S. teens enjoy many rights that are not extended to their peers in other countries.

Contraception, pregnancy, abortion, and adoption have become important issues for many U.S. teens.

Children rescued from child traffickers sat with security in China in April 2006.

Trafficking:
Modern Slave Trading

lthough slavery is illegal, traffickers still capture and sell at least 600,000 human beings a year on the international market. Women and children are most vulnerable, although men are also at risk. Female slaves usually end up in brothels or as laborers in sweatshops. Sometimes they become prisoner-wives or servants in private homes. Male slaves are usually forced to work on farms or in the restaurant business.

SLAVES IN CHINA

China is one of the major destinations for trafficked girls and women. This is because of China's policy allowing only one child per family. The one-child rule was enacted in 1979 because China was extremely overpopulated, but the law had unforeseen consequences. Traditionally, Chinese boys care for their parents in old age. If parents can only have one child, they often prefer to have a son. Ultrasound tests can determine if a fetus is male or female well before birth. If the fetus is female, couples frequently decide to abort the pregnancy and try again for a boy. Now girls of marriageable age are in short supply, so they are being imported from other countries.

The Worst Offenders

In 2008, the United States government named 14 countries as Tier 3 nations. This means those countries are the worst offenders for human trafficking and not making any meaningful efforts to rectify the situation. Those countries are Kuwait, Oman, Qatar, Saudi Arabia, Algeria, Burma, Cuba, Fiji, Iran, Moldova, North Korea, Papua New Guinea, Sudan, and Syria.

Traffickers may capture their victims by force, but vulnerable people are often lured by false job offers. In China, organized trafficking rings capture teenage girls by going to poor villages and pretending to be recruiters for employers in other districts. They offer the girls well-paying jobs as nannies or factory workers. Once the girls reach their destinations, they discover they are not at a job site. Instead, they are auctioned off to the highest bidder. Many of them end up as the unwilling wives of old or disabled men who could not find women willing to marry them. Human trafficking occurs everywhere—including the Middle East, Asia, Russia, and the United States.

Trafficked Products

Some products found in the United States may contain ingredients that were created by trafficked victims. One of the most common of these is chocolate. By purchasing chocolate products, consumers may be unwillingly supporting human trafficking.

Chocolate is made from cocoa, which is harvested on plantations. The world's largest producer of cocoa is Cote d'Ivoire, a country in Africa. Many of the workers on cocoa plantations in that country are young children, and many are forced to live and work in slave-like conditions. They work 12-hour days in the hot sun and are not given sufficient clothing, food, shelter, and rest.

Many stores carry what is called Fair Trade chocolate. If a product has the Fair Trade label, it means that those who produced it received fair wages and worked in fair conditions. By purchasing Fair Trade products, consumers can be sure that they are not supporting modern-day slavery.

Trafficking in the United States

Estimates vary, but the U.S. government believes that between 14,500 and 17,500 slaves end up in the United States each year. Although the practice is more common overseas, U.S. girls have also been kidnapped in their hometowns and sold into slavery. Most of the people trafficked each year in the United States are women and children who become household servants or are forced into the sex industry. The men who are trafficked are used as construction or agricultural laborers. Often they are migrant laborers, which means they travel from job to job. Migrant laborers are vulnerable to exploitation because they often do not speak English. Employers who see an easy way to profit can underpay migrant workers or fail to pay them at all. The United States passed the Trafficking Victims Protection Reauthorization Act in 2005 to deal with problems such as these.

Do Trafficked Victims Ever Escape?

Rarely trafficked victims do escape, but most never see their families again. Jailers debilitate slaves through several methods, making it difficult for them to flee. For example, captives are often deliberately traumatized, usually by rape, beatings, starvation, and threats of violence. Through fear, jailers gain obedience. Prisoners who remain disobedient are sometimes punished in front of the others to serve as an example.

Addictive drugs may also be used to keep victims dazed and calm. Drugs reduce the victims' ability to think clearly, so they cannot plan, look for opportunities to escape, or run away.

Many traffickers use psychological manipulation to control their captives. They may lie, make false promises, or threaten to hurt the victim's family. These tactics create fear in the victims, which may keep them compliant.

Seeking Help from Police

Many factors prevent trafficking victims from going to the police. Often they have been transported to foreign countries, where they do not speak the language. This, along with the fact that they did not enter the country legally, keeps them from seeking help from authorities. The problem is complicated by the fact that authorities tend to treat trafficked people as illegal immigrants, not taking into consideration that they were forced into

*Children in India participated in a silent protest
against human trafficking in January 2008.*

the country. U.S. immigration officials arrest and
deport illegal immigrants, forcing them to leave
the United States. Illegal immigrants might want
to avoid deportation, not only because conditions
in their native countries are bad, but also because
deportation separates them from friends or family
still in their new country.

In certain countries, the authorities cannot
be trusted. Some police officers and government
officials are in league with traffickers. Slavery
is a profitable business, and organized crime is

Staying Out of Danger

1. Never accept gifts from strangers. Kidnappers use gifts as bait.
2. Abductors can get close to children by asking them for help. Do not be fooled by this ploy.
3. Kidnappers threaten victims to get them to enter a vehicle quietly. The time to fight is before getting in the car, not once the vehicle reaches a remote location.
4. Many child molesters are not strangers. Children should tell parents if anyone ever touches them inappropriately.
5. "Too good to be true" offers of jobs, food, nice clothes, and travel should be treated with suspicion. People making these offers may be traffickers.

sometimes involved. Groups such as the Mafia have been known to pay off or threaten police officers so they can do business without interference.

TRAFFICKING OF CHILDREN

Like adult slaves, children are sometimes kidnapped. But children face a unique threat. They may be sold into slavery by their desperately poor parents.

Child slaves may become laborers or household servants, as is common in Central America. They may be forced into prostitution or used to make child pornography. Some pedophiles, or adults who have an abnormal sexual attraction to children, will pay to molest a child.

Thailand is known as a destination for "child sex tourists," pedophiles who want to have sex with very young children. In Thailand, as in the United States, pedophiles are prosecuted and jailed if convicted.

Other trafficked children are illegally sold to adoption agencies. Guatemala and India are two countries where abducted babies are reportedly put up for adoption. The adoption agencies charge large fees to couples from Western countries, claiming that the money pays for lawyers' costs and the expenses of the birth mother. These couples are told that children at the orphanage were freely given up for adoption, but some new parents unknowingly take home kidnapped children.

CLEVER KIDNAPPERS

Kidnappers can be extremely manipulative. In order to lure victims, they may stage a scene where they seem as if they need help. For example, a kidnapper may stop on the side of the road and pretend to have a flat tire. They count on the fact that people will stop to help, and when someone does, they may attack the person.

In other instances, the kidnapper may cause someone trouble so as to appear as a rescuer. For example, a victim may find a flat tire or other problem on his or her own vehicle.

Child Pornography

Child pornography is illegal. It exploits children by circulating naked or sexual images of them, usually via the Internet. Sometimes children are videotaped being molested. The tapes are then sold to pedophiles. Children suffer lasting emotional and physical damage from being sexually exploited. Law enforcement authorities survey Internet sites to try to catch child pornographers and rescue exploited children.

A kidnapper may just "happen" to be driving by and stop to help. The kidnapper can then gain the person's trust or gratitude, making way for an easy attack.

Was Natalee Holloway Trafficked?

In 2005, American Natalee Holloway disappeared on the island of Aruba during her senior class trip. She was never seen again. One suspect in the case is Dutch citizen Joran van der Sloot, who was the last person seen with Natalee. He was arrested twice in connection with her disappearance, but both times he was released due to insufficient evidence.

In an exposé, an undercover operative met with Van der Sloot in Thailand. The operative, posing as a sex-industry kingpin, videotaped Van der Sloot. He was promising that he could sell Thai girls as sex slaves. His plan was to tell them they were going to Holland to work as dancers. Reportedly, Van der Sloot makes the equivalent of approximately $13,000 for each Thai girl he traffics. Investigators wonder if Van der Sloot sold Natalee into slavery and whether she is still alive.

KIDNAPPE

LAST SEEN AT CARLOS & CHARLIES
MONDAY, MAY 29, 2005 1:30AM
NATALEE HOLLOWAY
CAUCASIAN AMERICAN FEMALE
BLUE EYES / LONG BLOND HAIR
5'4" 110 LBS.   18 YEARS OLD

ANY INFORMATION
PLEASE CALL 587-6222
OR CALL POLICE STATION 1

This poster was created and released by the family of U.S. teen Natalee Holloway following her disappearance in Aruba in 2005.

A Pakistani man holds his seven-year-old son, right, and his son's four-year-old "bride," left. Her father sold her to make money.

CHILDREN FORCED
TO MARRY

Child marriage is defined as the marriage of any person, male or female, who is under the age of 18. Marriages of children are often arranged by their parents, so the young people most likely have no input on the choice of their spouse.

In some countries, it is not unusual for a young bride to see her groom for the first time at the wedding ceremony. Such marriages are in violation of basic human rights.

Why Child Marriages Occur

Early marriages are cultural traditions in Afghanistan, Bangladesh, Ethiopia, Pakistan, India, and the Middle East. In these countries, it is not unusual for nine- or ten-year-old girls to marry, but 16 is a more common age. Human rights activists are most opposed to marriages of prepubescent children.

Dowries are traditional in India and other areas of South Asia. A dowry is a payment, in goods or money, usually paid to the bride's family by the groom's family. The dowry compensates the family of the bride for the loss of their daughter's household help. In higher social classes, the payments may be reversed

Honor Killings

In some parts of the Muslim world, women and girls can be killed for any perceived dishonor to their families. Often it is their fathers or brothers who carry out the death sentence. Honor killings occur for offenses such as refusal to agree to an arranged marriage, divorcing a husband (even in cases of extreme abuse), or being raped. Rape victims are considered guilty for "permitting" themselves to be raped—even if they fought back. Men who commit honor killings are rarely prosecuted and even more rarely convicted. However, Islamic law does not approve such murders.

with the bride's family paying the groom's because wealthy women do not work.

A dowry is substantial, so a young man must work and save for many years to afford one. Consequently, husbands tend to be much older than their wives. Poor families are sometimes induced to marry off their daughters at young ages in order to receive dowries.

In many cultures, it is important for a girl to be a virgin at her marriage, especially in the Middle East. The loss of a girl's virginity outside marriage is considered a dishonor to her entire family. Younger girls are thought more likely to be virgins than older ones, so men prefer very young

A Child Bride Resists

Nujood Ali was one of 16 children in a family of beggars from Yemen, a country in the Middle East. She was only ten years old when her father arranged her marriage to a 30-year-old man. This is not illegal in Yemen, where the average bride is 12 or 13. Nujood did not want to get married, but she had no choice.

No one had taught her anything about sexual intercourse. On her wedding night, she was scared and confused. When her new husband took off her clothes, she ran away, frightened and sobbing. He caught her, raped her, and then beat her up. That was the first of many beatings she would suffer. She complained to her father, but he did not help her. A divorce would dishonor her entire family. Although women in Yemen did not usually go out of the house without a man, she went alone to the courthouse. The judge heard her story and granted her an immediate divorce. She became a celebrity in her country and a symbol for Yemeni activists working to end childhood marriage.

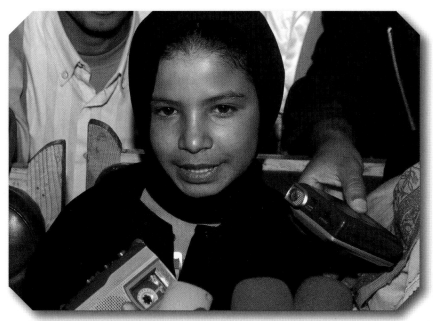

In April 2008, Nujood Ali spoke to the press about how her unemployed father forced her into an arranged marriage.

brides. If a Middle Eastern girl is known not to be a virgin, even because she was raped, the chances of her marrying are very small. Families worry that such misfortune will befall their daughters and so they push for early marriages.

In Africa, human immunodeficiency virus (HIV) and acquired immunodeficiency syndrome (AIDS) are huge health issues. There is a myth that an HIV-positive man will be cured if he has sex with a virgin. The idea encourages men to marry children. It also leads to the infection of countless young girls with the lethal HIV virus.

Physical Damage Done by Early Marriage

Child marriages harm girls' bodies in many ways. Though girls enter puberty and become physically capable of becoming pregnant, they are not yet fully grown. If a child bride becomes pregnant, the pregnancy is very risky for both her and her baby. Often the girl's pelvis is not large enough for a baby to pass through during childbirth, and the baby becomes trapped in the birth canal. This is called obstructed labor. It can be fatal to both the mother and the baby, and those young mothers who do survive it suffer severe physical damage.

Babies of adolescent mothers have a higher risk of health problems or death than those of older girls or women. Girls normally grow until

Obstetric Fistulas

An obstetric fistula is a rupture, or hole, in the wall of the vagina or rectum, caused by obstructed labor. During childbirth, the uterus contracts powerfully. If the woman's pelvis is too narrow for the baby to pass through, the uterus will still continue to contract, leading to a rupture. Fistulas are avoidable by prompt medical attention during childbirth. A Cesarean section, where the baby is surgically removed, is one solution. Those who have fistulas often have embarrassing losses of bladder and bowel control. Fistulas can be repaired with surgeries.

In March 2009, victims of forced marriage attended school in Burkina Faso, a country in western Africa.

they are 17 or 18. Their growing bodies require much energy already. They cannot also accommodate the energy pregnancy requires, especially in developing countries where nutrition is likely to be poor. The growth of both the young mother and her baby can be stunted.

Young brides often have no access to birth control and begin having babies early. In addition, they have a much higher rate of HIV and sexually transmitted diseases than unmarried girls. The brides are infected by their husbands, who, in turn, were infected by another sexual partner. Husbands in male-dominated cultures often have girlfriends, though they demand that their wives remain faithful.

EARLY MARRIAGE MEANS LOST OPPORTUNITIES

Men and women in developed countries often share household chores. However, in places where child marriage is practiced, men and women tend to have very separate roles. Usually men work outside the home, and women are responsible for household chores and child rearing. This destroys educational opportunities for young wives, because they must leave school to take care of the home. Their limited education restricts them to low-paying jobs, if they can get a job outside the home at all. Many husbands discourage their wives from finding such jobs.

Child Brides in the United States

A polygamous Mormon sect is a religious community that allows a man to marry more than one wife. In 2008, five members of such a group faced child sex abuse charges for arranging illegal "spiritual" marriages of girls as young as 12 to sect leaders. Some of the men had as many as ten wives. The male-dominated religious community taught women that they were the property of their husbands and must obey them to please God. Warren Jeffs, the sect leader, had a 14-year-old wife whom he had married two years before the abuses became public. He was found guilty of multiple charges and is serving a lengthy prison sentence.

Usually, a child wife is financially dependent upon her husband and may become isolated from her family and friends. If the husband is abusive, she has few options. With little money and few prospects of getting a job, a young wife is likely to stay in an abusive marriage.

PREVENTING CHILD MARRIAGE

The United Nations Children's Fund (UNICEF), a human rights organization, advocates education to eliminate the practice of child marriage. Studies have shown that educated girls are likely to marry later and have a higher standard of living than uneducated girls. They also are more likely to have healthier and fewer babies than girls who left school early.

Families in developing countries tend to leave sons in school longer than daughters, because girls are expected to perform most of the

HPV and Cervical Cancer

The Human Papillomavirus (HPV) is transmitted sexually. Health care workers have discovered that child brides are likely to contract this virus from their husbands. HPV causes genital warts, which may or may not be visible. The virus also causes cancer of the cervix, which can be fatal if not discovered early. HPV can be prevented with a vaccine.

household chores. UNICEF supports leaving daughters in school. It also promotes education for girls on the prevention of pregnancy and sexually transmitted diseases. The organization is working to develop social support networks to house and protect girls who flee from forced marriages. ⌒

These eight-year-olds were engaged in Jordan in January 1996. The
engagement was imposed on them by their parents.

العنف الكلامي

A girl participated in a protest against child violence and child sexual
abuse in Beirut, Lebanon, in November 2008.

SEXUAL ABUSE
OF CHILDREN

ost children know that inappropriate
touching of genital or breast areas or
sexual intercourse between an adult and a child are
forms of sexual abuse. But not all forms of child
sex abuse involve touching. For example, if an adult

makes sexually suggestive comments to a child, ridicules an adolescent's developing body, or asks prying questions about previous sexual experiences, this is sexual abuse. Exposing part or all of an adult's naked body to a child or showing children sexually explicit images is also sexual abuse. All of these forms of abuse are illegal, even if the adult convinces the child to participate.

Sex abusers can molest children by force. Others gradually convince victims that sexual activity is all right, even though it is not. If in doubt, secrecy is one sure sign that a crime was committed. If the adult had done nothing wrong, it would not need to be kept secret.

VICTIMS AND PERPETRATORS

In the United States, one in every four girls and one in every six boys will become a victim of child sex abuse by the age of 18. Child molesters can be men or women, but most of them are men. They might even be teens or children only a few

Physical Signs of Past Sexual Abuse

Not all children who have been sexually abused show signs of injury, but some do. Possible injuries resulting from rape or molestation include bleeding or scrapes around the mouth, anus, or genitals. Another sign of past abuse is a discharge or bad odor from the genitals, which might be a symptom of a sexually transmitted disease. Because most abused children will not speak out, parents, doctors, and siblings who are alert for these signs may help rescue them.

years older than their victims. Some of them are trusted people in their communities, such as priests or teachers. Not all abuse is perpetrated by strangers. In many cases, the abuser is a caregiver or even the victim's parent. Child sex abusers are strangers only 10 to 15 percent of the time.

Pedophiles might initially gain a child's trust with gifts, fun outings, or unconditional emotional support. They often befriend parents too, so that the parents trust them around their children. Once in a position of trust, an abuser might tell the victim that he or she is special. The abuser will then try to make the child believe that sexual activity is a secret sign of their loving bond.

No single child is likely to be truly special to a molester, because each molester typically victimizes many children. On average, pedophiles who target girls abuse 50 girls before being arrested. Because boys report molestation more rarely than girls, pedophiles who victimize boys abuse approximately 150 boys before they are caught.

Psychological Results of Sexual Abuse

About half of the survivors of sexual abuse develop post-traumatic stress disorder (PTSD). People with PTSD relive the bad event repeatedly in memory and avoid things associated with the abuser or the event. Many PTSD children are hyperactive, which means they are extremely jumpy and tend to suffer episodes of heart-pounding fear if startled. Even after they become adults, they are likely to suffer from depression, anxiety, and health problems.

ABDUCTIONS BY STRANGERS

Sexual predators who kidnap their victims are more likely to kill them than predators who have first developed relationships with their victims. However, abductions of children by strangers are quite rare.

It is important for children to realize that they do not have to obey strangers, especially if the stranger is ordering them to do something frightening, such as getting into a vehicle or walking to a deserted place. Parents and teachers train children to obey adults, even when children do not want to. The adults' intention is to make kids well behaved, but kidnappers can take advantage of this to get children into vehicles without a fight.

Abductors make death threats to get their victims to come quietly. But going with the kidnapper is riskier than fighting. Kidnappers do not want to create a scene and become noticed by people in the area. A child who makes a lot of noise is more likely to escape and survive than one who meekly complies.

The 2004 Murder of Carlie Brucia

When a kidnapper grabbed 11-year-old Carlie Brucia at a car wash in 2004, his crime was caught on tape by surveillance cameras. Carlie was walking home from a friend's house and decided to take a shortcut through a car wash. Though the man held her arm, the blonde sixth-grader got into his vehicle without a struggle. Acquaintances who saw the televised tapes recognized the kidnapper as mechanic Joe Smith. He is now in jail for kidnapping, sexual battery, and the first-degree murder of Carlie Brucia.

A child who uses physical violence to avoid abduction or molestation will not get in trouble at school or with the law because the violence is self-defense.

Generally, the longer a child is with an abductor, the lower the chance of his or her escaping alive. Abducted kids should make every effort to escape as soon as possible.

CHILD PORNOGRAPHY

Child pornography shows children performing sex acts or posing naked or partially clothed. It is a large industry. Photos and videotapes are bought and sold all over the world. In some particularly disturbing instances, the children are

Catching the Predators

The Federal Bureau of Investigation (FBI) works to identify and arrest child pornographers and to free exploited children. One tactic used by the FBI is to set up fake links to supposed child pornography sites. When a person clicks on the link, even from a private home computer, the FBI can trace the connection to the computer that sent it. They can then determine who was using the computer and make the arrest. Possessing child pornography, even if made by other people, is illegal.

In another sting operation, police officers pose as children over the phone or the Internet. When the pedophiles show up in person, expecting to meet the child, they are arrested.

A popular television show called *To Catch a Predator* documents this kind of operation. The predator walks into the home where he is planning to meet the child. Instead, he meets the host of the show, Chris Hansen. Camera crews document the predator's reaction. Hansen stated, "There's no way of knowing how aggressive they might get when they see me instead of a young teenager, and when they realize they will be exposed on [television]."[1]

photographed or videotaped while being tortured, raped, or forced to hurt other children. People who want to see such pictures are mentally disturbed and are likely to be child molesters themselves. It is a federal crime for anyone to possess or distribute child pornography, but the children involved are considered victims. They would not be prosecuted for their part in the crime.

CHILD PROSTITUTES

Many runaways are children who were victims of incest at home. The Children of the Night organization was established to rescue children from prostitution. According to the organization, sexually abused children react differently in conflict situations than other children do. Most have little aggression and cannot defend themselves. Compliance was a survival strategy in the abusive home, and it makes runaways victims on the street too. They are easy targets for pimps who profit by forcing other people into prostitution.

Escape from Prostitution

Underage prostitutes who want to leave the sex trade can call Children of the Night's 24-hour hotline at 1-800-551-1300. Volunteers will arrange free transportation and shelter. The organization will also help with the transition back to school and a stable life either at home or in foster care.

Actress Jamie Lee Curtis participates in the Commitment to Kids campaign, which helps keep children safe.

Pimps line up customers for their prostitutes, but they keep most of the money that is made. They use physical and emotional abuse to keep their girls, and sometimes boys, working for them.

Underage girls and boys are trafficked by their pimps throughout the United States. Once they are separated from their families and friends, they have few options. Even if they could return home, some street kids believe that their families would not want them back because they were prostitutes. In the vast majority of cases, families of such children *do* want them back and are still searching for them many years after they disappear. Police stations or social service agencies can help runaways return home. Social services can also arrange safe foster care, so if the original home was abusive, runaways can still get off the streets.

VICTIMS CAN TAKE CONTROL

Children who have been molested are often reluctant to report the crime because telling the story forces them to relive the experience. However, the best way for children to stop child molesters is to speak out. Molesters try to make their victims feel responsible. They play on the victims' fear and shame to keep them quiet. But victims of child sex abuse are not guilty of any crime. Young people who have been violated should tell a trusted adult. Or they can call the police themselves by dialing 911.

From Prostitute to Community Organizer

When Carissa Phelps was abandoned at the age of 12 by her mother, she was placed in a group home. She eventually ran away. Alone on the streets, she got hungry. A man bought her a hot dog and a soda. Then he raped her and forced her into prostitution. Years later, after a conviction for stealing a car, Carissa decided to change her life. She was tired of living in fear. Now, after graduating from business school and law school, she is back in her old neighborhood, working to make it a better place. A documentary movie was made about her life.

Compassionate and experienced officers will listen
and take appropriate measures to stop molesters.

Internet Safety for Kids

The Internet is a common way for pedophiles
to meet children, so young people must be wary
online. Criminals visit chat rooms designed for kids
and pose as young people. They use text-message
abbreviations, current slang, and even insert spelling
mistakes so they seem like kids.

Innocent-sounding information that kids send
to each other, such as their names, hometowns, or
what schools they attend, can provide a predator with
the clues he needs to find his next victim. Phone
numbers should be kept confidential and only given
to friends during face-to-face conversations. This
is important because reverse phone books on the
Internet provide addresses when phone numbers are
entered. No one should ever give out photos or any
personal information to anyone on the Internet.

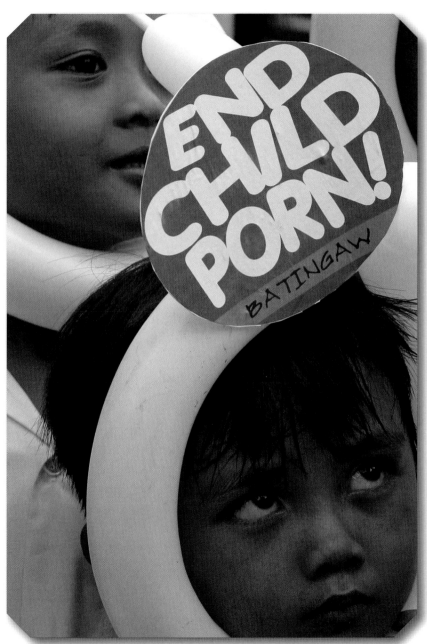

*Filipino children participated in a rally denouncing
child pornography in September 2007.*

Child soldiers in Uganda

CHILD SOLDIERS

ommanders of armies that use children as soldiers say that children are fearless fighters who obey orders without question. They do not expect to be paid as adult soldiers do. Their understanding of strategy and consequences is limited, so children will carry out very dangerous missions. The death rate of children in military organizations is high, but that is not of importance to their commanders. When those children die, the leaders will recruit or abduct others to replace them.

WHERE CHILDREN ARE SOLDIERS

In the United States and other developed countries, proof of age is required to join the military. But armies in many politically unstable nations do not require such documentation, even if the recruit is obviously a child. International law bans anyone under 18 from serving in the armed forces, but in war-torn regions these laws are almost impossible to enforce. Many countries—even those with many child soldiers—also have their own laws against enlisting minors, but the practice continues.

A 2007 U.S. State Department human rights report charged that the governments of Afghanistan, Burma,

UN Optional Protocol

The UN Convention on the Rights of the Child includes an optional protocol that bans the use of child soldiers. Signatory countries agree to ensure that all members of their militaries are at least 18 years old and enlist voluntarily. The agreement also requires nations to legally punish any non-state groups found to be using children as combatants. Currently, 121 countries have signed the optional protocol.

Chad, Democratic Republic of the Congo, Somalia,
Sri Lanka, Sudan, and Uganda were deliberately
recruiting children into their militaries. These
armies use younger children as cooks, laborers,
sentries, and spies. When the children grow strong
enough to carry a gun, even at nine or ten years old,
they become combatants.

Passing laws is not enough to stop the use of
children as soldiers. The problem is complicated
because in politically unstable countries not all
armies are controlled by the government. These
rebel military forces, referred to as non-state
groups, battle governments or each other. Non-state
groups are often made up of religious or political
fanatics. They do not feel obligated to follow laws
passed by the regimes they are resisting, especially
when governments do not follow the laws themselves.
In Africa, case studies have shown that government
forces and non-state groups are equally likely to use
child combatants.

How Children Become Soldiers

Poor or homeless children may enlist voluntarily
in the military, usually because armies promise them
food and shelter. Abused boys and girls might also

Child soldiers, including girls, of the Dac Cong special forces stand in uniform at an army base in Vietnam.

enlist to escape from bad home lives. However, most child soldiers are forced into the military.

For example, in Burma, a country in Southeast Asia, cash payments equaling about $32 are given to people who bring in child recruits. This induces corrupt people to bring in children against their will. Burmese police are said to sometimes detain street children and give them the choice of enlisting or being imprisoned.

In Africa, kidnapping is the most common way for children to join rebel armies. In one common

Patrick's Story

Fifteen-year-old Patrick of the Democratic Republic of the Congo was going to buy soap when rebel fighters caught him. The men took Patrick to a rebel base. He and other kidnapped children cared for the wounded and buried the dead. After only one week of military training, Patrick was sent into combat. He managed to slip away and flee to a UN outpost, where he was rescued but not returned home. Aid workers told Patrick that the rebels would likely find him and kill him for desertion if he returned to his village.

scenario, an armed force invades a village and separates possible combatants from those they deem useless as fighters. The captives, including children as young as seven, are conscripted into the army, while the rest are usually killed. Schools are another target of kidnappers. In 2001, an armed group abducted 60 Angolan children and a teacher from their school, probably for use as combatants, sex slaves, and servants in the army.

The Taliban is an extremely militant Islamic political group. In Pakistan, the Taliban has taken over some Islamic schools called *madrasas*. The Taliban uses the schools to spread its militant thinking and recruit suicide bombers. Students are lured with tales of the glory of self-sacrifice and then trained for suicide missions. In July 2007, security forces stopped a 14-year-old boy who had been sent across the border into Afghanistan to carry out a suicide attack on a provincial governor. The boy was considered a victim of the Taliban, so he was not punished and was returned to his home.

In another incident, Taliban militants tried to trick a child into being a suicide bomber. They placed an explosive vest on a six-year-old Afghan boy, telling him it would spray out flowers when he pushed a button. The boy sought help from government soldiers after he realized the vest was a bomb. The vest was safely removed and the child was not injured. Use of children in combat is against the published rules of the Taliban, but it happens nonetheless.

The Taliban

The Taliban is a fundamentalist Islamic movement fighting against both the Afghan government and North Atlantic Treaty Organization (NATO) forces. Its members are difficult to capture because they use guerilla tactics of attacking and then rapidly retreating to remote areas. The Taliban frequently uses suicide bombers who are motivated by the belief that martyrs are rewarded in heaven. Because the Taliban deliberately targets civilians, it is considered a terrorist organization.

The Taliban advocates a strict interpretation of Islamic religious law, which is very repressive to women. Until 2001, the Taliban ruled Afghanistan. During that time, Afghan women were banned from employment, even if they had no husband, father, or brother to support them. They were forced to wear burkas—robes that covered their heads and veiled their faces—when they left their homes. They were beaten with sticks by religious police if they did not comply. Under the Taliban, girls were not allowed to attend school past the age of eight, and many were forced into polygamous marriages at very young ages.

What Happens to Child Soldiers

Worldwide, militias that recruit child soldiers use similar training tactics. One of the first steps for turning a child into a willing killer is to break the child's bond with his home village or community. They may do this by forcing a young recruit to kill a fellow villager, usually in view of neighbors and relatives. If the child refuses, he is killed and the next recruit is given the same order. Former child soldier Ishmael Beah, who wrote a book about his experiences, says that children have been forced to kill their own families in order to prove their loyalty to the military. Villagers begin to hate and fear child soldiers, and they may not welcome the children back home if they do escape.

Beatings and harsh physical training are used to toughen the new recruits and numb them emotionally. Child soldiers in training are forced to watch or carry out acts of cruelty and are punished or threatened with death for crying. Recruits who obediently perform murders or other atrocities are praised by their commanders.

Because children are still developing psychologically, they are much easier to brainwash than adults. They also are more fragile emotionally and suffer lasting psychological damage from witnessing and carrying out acts of violence.

CHILD SOLDIERS ARE GIVEN DRUGS

Militias often use profits from drug smuggling to finance their war efforts. In Afghanistan, the Taliban grows opium poppies. These flowers are used to produce heroin, a dangerous addictive drug. Afghan heroin is sold primarily in Europe to addicts who unwittingly support terrorism. Similarly, militias in South America, especially Colombia, profit from growing coca plants that are used to make cocaine. Much of the illegal drug is sold to users in the United States.

When military organizations are involved with drug smuggling, drugs are cheap and easy for soldiers to get. Commanders sometimes drug child soldiers to hype them up for battle while reducing their natural pain and fear. Drug addiction is also a powerful motivator.

A 13-year-old Soldier

Djibril Karim was not abducted into the Sierra Leone Army; he joined voluntarily. He needed food and protection against rebel soldiers who attacked civilians. As adult soldiers were maimed or killed, the army recruited children to replace them. Some were so small that they could not carry their guns and had to drag them along through the dirt. To survive in battle, Djibril had to shoot rebel soldiers, including other children. UNICEF was able to free Djibril and hundreds of other child soldiers and send them to a rehabilitation camp.

DEMOBILIZING CHILD SOLDIERS

Demobilizing is the process of disbanding soldiers after a war and returning them home. Workers from aid organizations, such as United Nations Children's Fund (UNICEF), try to convince military leaders to release child soldiers and allow them to be taken to demobilization centers, even while the wars are still going on.

Demobilization centers provide counseling, education, and health care to child soldiers so they can recover from trauma and return to their homes. Most of the children have mental problems from the stress of war. They tend to act aggressively when upset, so counselors teach them nonviolent ways of handling disagreements.

UNICEF reports that the vast majority of demobilized child soldiers are accepted fully by their families and communities, despite any behavior problems. Acts they committed while they were soldiers are generally recognized as being the responsibility of adults in command. ⌐

Children have been used in militaries in places such as Iraq.

This 14-year-old fought in a militia for six years. He has been demobilized.

In Search of
Just Solutions

isagreements over children's rights often stem from differences between cultures. Some cultures, especially those of Africa, South Asia, and the Middle East, traditionally allow women and children fewer rights than men. But many cultures have begun to focus on the rights of vulnerable individuals. For example, the United States and European nations have a history of exploiting the weak, but they now are among the most equitable nations in terms of civil rights.

Industrialized nations export their cultures to the developing world. This occurs not only through films and products, but also through their influence at the United Nations. The body's member nations decided that the rights of children were too important to be determined by individuals, communities, or even entire nations. They decided that the rights of children should be determined by all the member nations working together. In this way, all children will have the same rights.

CULTURE CLASH

As supporters of children's rights make their influence felt, cultures

Breaking Taboo

Betty Makoni of Zimbabwe knows that her culture tends to turn a blind eye to violence against women. Sexual abuse and rape are common, and many men do not consider these major crimes. A cultural taboo prevents discussion of the issue. Makoni started the Girl Child Network to raise awareness of the problems girls and women face in Zimbabwe. This activism is dangerous, especially because Makoni exposes the crimes of high-ranking men. She has been harassed, threatened, and arrested. In 2008, Makoni won Amnesty International USA's Ginetta Sagan Award for Women's and Children's Rights.

sometimes come into conflict. People who have followed traditional ways of life for generations are not always happy about outsiders telling them to change. For example, the tradition of child labor evolved as a strategy to help struggling communities survive. Some individuals in those communities may not be open to suggestions that their ways are wrong. Activists working to protect children sometimes put themselves in great personal danger because of this cultural backlash. One such activist was Iqbal Masih.

A French Activist against Mutilation

Linda Weil-Curiel is a French attorney and activist working to stop the tradition of female genital mutilation, an ancient practice designed to suppress a woman's sexuality by removing her external genitalia. It is practiced in sub-Saharan Africa and the Middle East, where female chastity is considered very important. Because sexual contact is painful for women who have undergone the procedure, the mutilation is believed to prevent them from having illicit affairs.

In this procedure, most or all of a female's external genitalia is cut off. It is done either by family members at home or as part of a village's coming-of-age ceremonies. The excruciating procedure occurs under non-sterile conditions and without painkillers. Girls who have been cut in this way have long-term problems with infections and may die. Once they are adults, intercourse is painful and problems occur during childbirth.

Thanks in part to Weil-Curiel's efforts, the practice is now illegal in France, and parents who force genital mutilation upon their daughters can be sentenced to prison. Women fleeing from planned mutilations for themselves or their daughters can now receive asylum in France, meaning they do not have to return home.

Iqbal's Story

In Pakistan in 1986, Saif Masih had a problem. His oldest son was about to be married. It was Pakistani custom for the father of the groom to pay for a share of the ceremony. The only thing Saif had that was worth any money was his four-year-old son, Iqbal. He traded Iqbal to a local *thekedar*, a man who ran a carpet factory, in exchange for a loan. Saif did not need the permission of Iqbal's mother, because women in Pakistan have fewer rights than men.

The agreement was that Iqbal would be freed from bonded labor once he had worked off the balance of the loan, which originally totaled 600 rupees, the equivalent of about $12. When he started, Iqbal earned about 2 cents a day, and after six years of weaving carpet, he earned approximately 40 cents a day. However, the *thekedar* charged the Masih family for Iqbal's food and tools. He also fined Iqbal for misbehavior. Later, the family took out another loan. The balance increased over the years. By the time Iqbal was ten, his family owed 13,000 rupees, approximately $260.

Iqbal was tied to the floor in front of a loom and forced to knot carpets 14 hours a day. The dusty wool gave him chronic bronchitis; sitting hunched

Young Iqbal Masih, a former child slave, worked to free children who were forced into bonded labor.

over caused a permanent hump in his spine. Still, he had spirit, and he complained more than the other children. He was beaten with his carpet-knotting tool and hung upside down for protesting his harsh working conditions.

The carpet factory owner intentionally underfed his child workers in order to keep them from growing, because little fingers were better at working the looms. At age ten, Iqbal was less than four feet tall (1.2 m) and weighed approximately 60 pounds (27 kg), which is the size of an average six-year-old. Years of malnutrition and confinement had permanently stunted his growth.

After six years of imprisonment, Iqbal heard about a meeting of the Bonded Labor Liberation Front (BLLF). This organization worked to free child slaves and return them to schools. He slipped away and attended the rally. He learned that bonded labor had been outlawed in Pakistan and that the *thekedar* had no right to hold him. He decided not to return to work. The BLLF helped draft a document that proclaimed Iqbal's freedom. Iqbal presented it to the *thekedar* and was freed from the carpet factory.

The BLLF enrolled Iqbal in school, and he began to speak out against child slavery. Although he suffered pain from arthritis, he traveled to Europe and the United States and spoke at schools and rallies. Students his own age were shocked to see that he was half their size. Iqbal was a gifted speaker and began to receive media attention. Publicity about child labor in the manufacturing of Pakistani carpets

The RugMark Label

Consumers love the artistic beauty of Middle Eastern carpets, but they might not buy them because of their association with child labor. Rug buyers now can look for the RugMark label, which guarantees the carpet was made without child labor. This certification is available only to carpet factories that are open to inspection at any time. They never hire children, and each rug is marked so that it can be traced back to the loom where it was made.

caused the U.S. market for these carpets to collapse. Few consumers wanted carpets made by child slaves. The Pakistani carpet manufacturers were not pleased.

At age 12, Iqbal returned to Pakistan to visit his family and continue his work to free bonded laborers. Iqbal was killed in Pakistan on Easter Sunday 1995 by a man with a shotgun. The murder was never solved, but many believe it was carried out by an agent of the carpet industry.

Children Helping Children

Elizabeth Bloomer was in seventh grade when Iqbal Masih visited her school in the United States. His story made Elizabeth want to help other exploited children. Working with students and teachers, she helped raise more than $140,000 for the Iqbal Masih Educational Fund. The fund built the School for Iqbal, a special school in Pakistan for freed child laborers.

CHILDREN CAN MAKE A DIFFERENCE

Children can stand up for their own rights without starting their own aid organizations or going on speaking tours. People who are being treated unfairly have the right to set boundaries. Young people can say no to anyone who is taking advantage of them and seek help from trusted adults such as parents, teachers, or police.

Another way children can make a difference is by speaking out for others. Children sometimes

Children wearing masks participated in a run to mark World Day against Child Labor in Hyderabad, India, on June 12, 2008.

know about the mistreatment of other children, but they say nothing because they do not want to cause trouble. Speaking out is not causing trouble; it is the only real way to help. If one adult will not listen or will not take action, another should be told. Speaking out removes the power from abusers, who need secrecy to keep taking advantage of children.

Solving the Problem

Children's rights are supported in two ways. First, governments pass laws to protect children. Second,

A Young Hero

Craig Kielburger is an author and humanitarian who has spent most of his life helping children. His organization, Free the Children, recently sent large shipments of school supplies, blankets, and warm clothes to war-affected children in Afghanistan. The organization has also helped build more than 300 schools in rural areas of Africa. The schools provide education to some freed child soldiers. Kielburger has traveled all over the world in his mission to help children.

activists make sure that the laws are enforced. Activists push cultures to change by working directly with people in affected communities. In Pakistan, they freed Iqbal by letting him know that it was against the law for him to be enslaved.

Throughout the centuries, children have been victimized for cheap labor, the sex trade, and military gain. But children are not always voiceless. Along with adult activists, they have stood up to governments, political figures, and wealthy factory owners in order to secure their rights. That work is continuing today. As human rights activist Carol Bellamy said, "[I]n serving the best interests of children, we serve the best interests of all humanity."[1] ⁓

Children participated in a candlelight vigil organized for the elimination of child labor in Hyderabad, India, in June 2008.

TIMELINE

27 BCE– 476 CE

Fathers can legally sell and kill their children in the Roman Empire.

400–1400

European children can no longer be legally killed by their parents.

1760

The Industrial Revolution initiates a period of some of the worst abuses of child labor.

1842

The Coal Mines Act bans women and children from working in mines in Britain.

1904

The National Child Labor Committee mobilizes the anti-child labor movement in the United States.

1802

The British parliament limits the workday of child laborers to no more than 12 hours.

1834

Workhouses are introduced in Britain. They provide food and lodging in return for long work hours by the poor, both adults and children.

1842

R. H. Franks investigates working conditions of children employed in coal mines in Scotland.

1916 and 1918

U.S. laws banning child labor are passed but are declared unconstitutional by the Supreme Court.

1924

Congress passes a constitutional amendment banning child labor, but the bill is not ratified by the states.

TIMELINE

1938	1960	1979
U.S. President Franklin Delano Roosevelt signs the Fair Labor Standards Act.	The birth control pill becomes available in the United States.	China enacts the one-child policy.

1996	1996	2005
The United States passes a federal law making it illegal to perform any type of female genital mutilation or female circumcision.	A scandal surrounding Kathie Lee Gifford's clothing line publicizes the use of child labor to manufacture goods for U.S. markets.	The United States passes the Trafficking Victims Protection Reauthorization Act to deal with large-scale trafficking problems.

1989

The UN adopts its Convention on the Rights of the Child.

1995

Former child laborer and activist Iqbal Masih is killed in Pakistan.

2005

U.S. citizen Natalee Holloway disappears during a vacation in Aruba. Some believe she was kidnapped and trafficked.

2007

A U.S. State Department report charges that the governments of eight countries are recruiting children into their militaries.

2008

Betty Makoni wins Amnesty International USA's Ginetta Sagan Award for Women's and Children's Rights.

ESSENTIAL FACTS

AT ISSUE

❖ The United Nations has taken steps to outline the rights of all children. Differing views each culture holds about the rights and roles of children make this task difficult. For example, some countries accept children marrying at very young ages, while others consider this practice wrong.

❖ Children have worked throughout history. In ancient times, they were considered the property of their fathers, and any money they earned went to their fathers. In medieval times, children were expected to help on farms to produce successful crops. During the Industrial Revolution, children often worked in factories to help their families survive.

❖ Historically, children have not had the same rights as adults. In the United States, children are required to attend school until eighth grade. Their relationships, religion, and clothing can be legally regulated by adults.

❖ Trafficking of children is a global problem. Children are bought and sold like slaves and forced to work for little or no pay. Their small size and nimble fingers make them ideal workers in trades such as weaving and sewing, but their working conditions are oppressive and often dangerous.

❖ Children around the world are often exploited through the sex industry. Some are forced to work as sex slaves or forced into child pornography.

❖ Because of tradition, some cultures force children to marry at a very early age. This can be physically and psychologically damaging to children.

❖ In nations around the world, children are forced to become soldiers. In many countries, this practice is illegal. However, child soldiers are often part of rebel armies, making the practice difficult to regulate.

CRITICAL DATES

Approximately 1760

The Industrial Revolution began. During this time, children worked in factories, mines, and other unsafe places. They were given minimal pay and worked in hazardous and unhealthy conditions.

1802

British parliament passed legislation limiting the workday. Children were not allowed to work more than 12 hours per day.

1989

The United Nations adopted a document that outlined the rights of all children under the age of 18. This document is named the Convention on the Rights of the Child.

2005

The United States passed legislation that dealt with international trafficking problems.

QUOTES

"Most of the [child] work force comes from underdeveloped or poverty-stricken areas. Some children are even sold by their parents, who often don't have any idea of the [terrible] working conditions."—*Hu Xingdau, economics professor at the Beijing Institute of Technology*

"[I]n serving the best interests of children, we serve the best interests of all humanity."—*Carol Bellamy, human rights activist*

ADDITIONAL RESOURCES

SELECT BIBLIOGRAPHY

Bergmann, Barbara R. *In Defense of Affirmative Action.* New York, NY: BasicBooks, 1996.

Freedman, Russell. *Kids at Work: Lewis Hine and the Crusade Against Child Labor.* New York, NY: Clarion Books, 1994.

King, Gilbert. *Woman, Child for Sale.* New York, NY: Chamberlain Bros., 2004.

O'Reilly, Bill. *Kids are Americans Too.* New York, NY: HarperCollins Publishers, 2007.

Parker, David L. *Before Their Time: The World of Child Labor.* New York, NY: The Quantuck Lane Press, 2007.

FURTHER READING

Crofts, Andrew. *The Little Hero–One Boy's Fight for Freedom: Iqbal Masih's Story.* Chicago, IL: Independent Publisher's Group, 2006.

Ensalaco, Mark. *Children's Human Rights: Progress and Challenges for Children Worldwide.* Lanham, MD: Rowman & Littlefield Publishers, 2005.

Reed, Jennifer. *Elizabeth Bloomer: Child Labor Activist.* Farmington Hills, MI: KidHaven Press, 2007.

WEB LINKS

To learn more about children's rights, visit ABDO Publishing Company online at **www.abdopublishing.com**. Web sites about children's rights are featured on our Book Links page. These links are routinely monitored and updated to provide the most current information available.

FOR MORE INFORMATION

For more information on this subject, contact or visit the following organizations.

Botto House/American Labor Museum
83 Norwood Street, Haledon, NJ 07508
973-595-7953
www.passaiccountynj.org/ParksHistorical/Historical_Attractions/bottohouse.htm
This museum chronicles the history of child labor and the labor movement.

The Gaston County Museum
131 West Main Street, Dallas, NC 28034
704-922-7681
www.gastoncountymuseum.org
The Gaston County Museum features exhibitions of mill town life and Lewis Hine's photography.

Kidpower International
P.O. Box 1212, Santa Cruz, CA 95061
800-467-6997
www.kidpower.org
Kidpower International offers workshops that teach children confidence-building skills to avoid abduction, abuse, and assault.

GLOSSARY

abduction
> The act of capturing and holding a person by force and against his or her will.

bonded labor
> A form of modern slavery in which the long-term labor of a captive worker is exchanged for a loan.

brothel
> A place where prostitutes work.

chattel
> An item of personal property.

conscription
> Enlistment by force, especially into a militia or other military group.

consent
> To agree to something.

consumers
> People who purchase goods and services.

corporal punishment
> The infliction of pain as a form of discipline.

foster care
> Temporary housing, meals, and parenting provided to a child who is not the biological child of the caregivers.

human trafficking
> The buying and selling of humans for purposes of forced labor or sexual exploitation.

incest
> Sexual activity between two people who are closely related to each other.

insignia
> A mark or a sign affiliated with a certain group.

manipulation
The act of influencing another person using deceit for the purpose of personal gain.

minimum age of consent
The age at which a person can legally agree to have sex.

molestation
Sexual abuse in which an older or stronger person touches a child sexually or forces the child to perform sex acts.

pedophiles
People with an abnormal sexual attraction to children.

prepubescence
A stage of a child's life that occurs before puberty.

prostitution
The act of performing sex acts for money or other items of value.

psychological damage
Trauma, lasting anxiety, aggression, or pain from a bad experience that affects future behavior and relationships.

reform
To improve an existing social or political system.

sweatshops
Factories that exploit laborers, making them work long hours in uncomfortable conditions for low pay.

taboo
A subject or an act that is seen as offensive or immoral by a certain culture.

unscrupulous
Without normal morals or principles; failing to adhere to community standards of right and wrong.

virgins
People who have never experienced sexual intercourse.

SOURCE NOTES

Chapter 1. Ashiq's Story

1. Stephanie Strom. "A Sweetheart Becomes Suspect: Looking beyond Those Kathie Lee Labels." *New York Times*. 27 June 1996. 27 Jan. 2009 <http://query.nytimes.com/gst/fullpage.html?res=980 3E0DA1239F934A15755C0A960958260&sec=&spon=&pagewan ted=2>.

2. David Barboza. "China Says Abusive Child Labor Ring Is Exposed." *New York Times*. 1 May 2008. 13 Feb. 2009 <http://www.nytimes.com/2008/05/01/world/asia/01china. html?pagewanted=1&_r=1>.

Chapter 2. History of Child Labor
1. John Simkin. "Lord Ashley." *Spartacus Educational*. 27 Jan. 2009
<http://www.spartacus.schoolnet.co.uk/IRashley.htm>.
2. R. H. Franks. "Sheriffhall and Somerside Collieries: Children's
Employment Commission 1842." 27 Jan. 2009 <http://www.
hoodfamily.info/docs/franksreport/sheriffhallsomerside.html>.
3. John Simkin. "Lord Ashley." *Spartacus Educational*. 27 Jan. 2009
<http://www.spartacus.schoolnet.co.uk/IRashley.htm>.

Chapter 3. Rights of U.S. Teens
None.

Chapter 4. Trafficking: Modern Slave Trading
None.

SOURCE NOTES CONTINUED

Chapter 5. Children Forced to Marry
None.

Chapter 6. Sexual Abuse of Children
1. "Behind-the-scenes of 'To Catch a Predator' III."
MSNBC.com. 3 Feb. 2006. 27 Jan. 2009 <http://www.msnbc.msn.com/id/11103248/>.

Chapter 7. Child Soldiers
None.

Chapter 8. In Search of Just Solutions
1. "Speeches—UNICEF Executive Board, September 1999."
UNICEF. 7 Sept. 1999. 13 Feb. 2009 <http://www.unicef.org/media/media_11984.html>.

INDEX

Index Continued

ABOUT THE AUTHOR

Courtney Farrell is the author of numerous books, encyclopedia entries, and magazine articles and has contributed to a dozen college-level textbooks. She lives with her husband and sons on a ranch in Colorado.

PHOTO CREDITS